YOU ARE NOT YOUR WRITING

WRITER CHAPS – SEASON ONE

SHORT BOOKS FULL OF OUTSTANDING ADVICE FROM AUSTRALIA'S TOP SPECULATIVE FICTION WRITERS

YOU ARE NOT YOUR WRITING

& Other Sage Advice

ANGELA SLATTER

Brain Jar Press
PO Box 6687
Upper Mt Gravatt, QLD, 4122
Australia
www.BrainJarPress.com

Cover design by Peter Ball
Cover Image: *Businesswoman in the workplace. Pop art retro*, studiostoks
/Shutterstock

ISBN: 9781922479044

Contents

How to Be A Writer

So I was supposed to be answering interview questions, but for some reason I wrote this. Everyone's experience and advice will be different, but this is mine.[1]

1. A writer writes (Thanks, *Throw Momma from the Train* and Sean Williams)

You write.

You apply the bum glue and you write.

You write no matter how attractive cleaning the toilet suddenly becomes, or how urgent clearing out the vegetable crisper seems or doing your tax or cutting your own hair (to note: that last one is an especially bad idea — why yes, I have done these stupid things so you don't have to).[2]

You write even though you are certain this is the worst thing you — or indeed anyone else on this planet or any other — have ever written.

You write.

Sure, writers have demons and inner critics that whisper horrible, discouraging things to us. But some of us give them undignified pet names and enrol them in short courses to get them off our hands … send them off to playgroups where they make children cry or rob banks.

The important thing is that **you** don't listen to them, or not everything at least. Listen to the reasonable stuff[3], but not the unreasonable ass-crazy stuff.[4]

There are ways to get through the writer's block (which is just fear spelled differently and with extra letters), and there are ways to finish stuff. The first step is telling the inner critic to shut the hell up when you're writing a first draft. A first draft doesn't need to be perfect, it just needs to *be*. A first draft is BrainVomit™ (thank you again, Sean Williams). So just write. Write garbage. All the spelling mistakes, all the grammatical errors (but take them out in future drafts — very important next yet-oft-forgot step).

Just breathe deeply and just write.

2. Be grateful

If someone has helped you along the way, be grateful. Acknowledge them publicly. You are no less a writer or creator of a story if you had assistance.

We all like to think this is an entirely solitary profession (and to some extent, sure, it is and it has to be because being surrounded by other people, especially ones you like, can be very distracting unless you're extremely disciplined). Part of the job *is* entirely solitary, but you don't create in a vacuum. You will help others and others will help you.

If you get to the point where you can do this as your full-time job, then be really grateful and never lose the memory of the times when you struggled. Don't go to festivals or book clubs and tell everyone how easy it was, that you encountered no obstacles, that no one helped you, don't tell everyone how fabulous and deserving of all this you are.

There are plenty of really good writers out there who don't get breaks or the chances, who don't get discovered. So, be humble, not an asshat.

Also be very aware that it might all change tomorrow. This is a snakes and ladders game; you might find yourself wishing you'd been more grateful to people who helped you early on when you were climbing the ladder now that you're on the snaky slippery-dip. There are more slowly starving mid-listers (although speeds may vary) than there are JK Rowlings with Scottish castles and unfortunate outlooks.

3. Networking is not a dirty word

Networking doesn't mean comparing business card sizes in a private club.

Join a writers' group. Find a mentor. Have beta-readers. Hold a weekly Write Club: Peter M. Ball and I have been doing this for about ten[5] years now.[6] Once a week we meet on a Wednesday, spend the first 30-45 minutes venting, exchanging market opportunities, offering support/sympathy, and advice on new projects and stalled ones. We also drink coffee. Then we start writing: two hours straight, then we have lunch and recalibrate, then two more hours of writing. It's not a social chat thing, it's a professional gathering with a friend. The work is primary.[7]

Networking is about building mutually beneficial relationships, not about getting as much out of other people as possible, or about you being the one doing ALL the favours. It's about building a community for yourself and others. I've said a lot of other stuff about networking for writers for Cultured Vultures, so get yourself a cuppa and a biscuit (okay, two biscuits) and have a read.[8]

4. Ditch your sense of entitlement

We write because if we don't, we explode. Our dreams turn sour (thanks, Meg Vann, for that one). No one asked you to do this job.

You're not entitled to a publishing contract or an award or even a viable career. This is not a job where you have staged promotions or pay increases. You don't have performance appraisals where someone in power pats you on the shoulder and says, 'Well done.' So, the sooner you let that expectation go, the happier you'll be.

Awards are a crap shoot: you have no guarantee of winning any during your career (or even being nominated for one), and they are basically nice statuettes and something a marketing department can use to help promote your next book. If you're really lucky, some have giant cheques attached (most don't). I've won awards and I've lost awards, and neither of those things have made me a better or worse writer.

Try to "future proof" your brain, by which I mean prepare for failure (don't expect it, but do have a back-up plan, just in case). There will be years, even for established writers, when you don't have good sales; when you write stories that no one except you loves. You might not have a novel coming out because of the vagaries of the industry; you will hear the phrase 'disappointing sales figures' from publishers who could not be fucked to do any marketing and promotion for your last book because they spent their entire budget on bus adverts for authors who can sell out with a single tweet. You will contemplate going back to a job in an office as a lampshade, or as a skunk wrangler.

But you will keep writing because a writer writes, and just because it feels like it's over, it's not over until the horizontally over-burdened lady sings. You keep writing because the next book will find someone who loves it. You will keep writing because you must have faith in yourself and what you do. You will keep writing because if you don't your head and heart will burst.

You will keep writing because the person you write for first and foremost is yourself, and you write because you cannot do anything else.

5. Practice makes almost-perfect

Nothing's ever perfect to the writer's mind, no matter how much readers love it.

We will always pick at what we've done (the nose isn't quite right, the left forearm is bigger than the right, there's a little bit of adjectival overload that I would totally not do now and OMG can I please re-edit that book from five years ago?). We'll never be entirely happy. Accept it.

For your own sanity there's a point where you must learn to let something go. I don't know what that point will be for you — *Fahrenheit 451?* — because every writer is different.

But if you are one day brooding darkly about how you're an unrecognised genius and no one's accepting your work for publication, then maybe check that you've actually sent some stuff out?

Rejection stings, but it should not destroy you or your joy in writing: just remember that not everyone is going to love everything you write. Either because it's not to their taste, or it's Tuesday, or their budgie died, or they're just being mean, or maybe there is a valid reason why your story is deeply inimical to their beliefs and is therefore not for them. You cannot follow all your readers home and explain everything to them (I think that's Le Guin paraphrased by Miéville): that's called stalking and it is (quite rightly) frowned upon.

You must learn to let go. *Whoosh.*

6. Be supportive

Just keep your pompoms at the ready and if someone has good news, then give them a big old 'Yay, you!' Don't leave comments on their Facebook posts along the lines of 'Congrats. Wish that had happened to me.' That's just, no. Don't. Don't hijack someone's joy. Just don't.

Another person's success takes nothing away from you (unless they published a book they stole from you, obviously, but that's outside the ambit of this post).

Be collegial: share open submissions posts (always with the caveat that individuals MUST do their own due diligence checks). Don't hoard opportunities, you're neither a miser nor a dragon (or you shouldn't be). If you've got nothing for an anthology but know someone who might be a good fit, then suggest them to the editor.

Beta-read for others, but don't always be the beta-reader — this needs to be an equal exchange of work. Two-way street, baby.

Don't have rivals. I run my own race, other people run theirs. I love their work and I'm happy to say so. Why wouldn't I be? More good writing out in the world? Thumbs up!

7. Be professional

Be organised and informed as a writer. Know the difference between sim-subs and multiple subs (equally as important in publishing as in BDSM circles). Read submission guidelines. Be aware of what rights you're selling or licensing.

Just because you've written "The End" doesn't mean your job is done. You've finished a first draft (Yay, you!), but now you need to let it lie fallow in the bottom drawer for two weeks (yes, a randomly chosen number) coz that gives you time to forget it. It gives you time to forget how brilliant and flawless you think it is. Put a bring-up date in your diary. Don't look at the story until then, although by all means write yourself post-it notes if you get ideas in the shower, etc (I do not recommend post-its in the shower, but I do suggest you keep some of those kids' crayons that write on tiles there). When your diary says 'Hey, it's time,' then get that story out and read it with fresh eyes. Cry. Regroup. Make the beverage of your choice. Begin the editing process. Don't use a red pen because then it looks like a nasty teacher has failed your assignment. Use blue or green. Unless of course you really love red pen, in which case, use the red pen.

This one is my bugbear and certain to send me into a rage: don't send a Like My Page request/demand after you've just sent someone a friend request on the Face of Book. And you know what? Think about it for a few months. See if you actually interact with that person, see if you like them, they like you. Have you read their books? Even then don't expect someone to come to the party.

Have you liked *their* page? Probably not. Yes, writers are also readers but they are probably not your primary target market — not least of all because we're all bloody impoverished and trying to sell our own books![9]

And seriously do not call someone out for not liking your page. This is the behaviour of a nutbar. Just don't do it. Remain polite at all times no matter how hard that might be. If in doubt, withdraw. There's an unfriend function for a reason.

8. Don't answer reviews

Even if you think the reviewer is entirely wrong-headed, wrong, unpleasant, drunk, stoned, vicious and vituperative, don't answer the review.

Again, there is also the horrible chance that they might be right …

If in doubt, take advice from Neil Gaiman (always a source of wisdom as well as excellent books) who says: 'When you publish a book — when you make art — people are free to say what they want about it. You can't tell people they liked a book they didn't like, and there is, in the end, no arguing with personal taste. Different people like different things. Best to move on and make good art as best you can, instead of arguing.' There's an even better one about just writing a new book that's so brilliant that critics and other writers will eviscerate themselves in despair but I couldn't find that one (so you get my crappy paraphrasing).

By all means, say whatever you want to your nearest and dearest. Rage, chew shoes, knock over rubbish bins and destroy newspapers. But do not go public. The internet never forgets. If you feel you must get it out of your system, then write it down on a piece of paper. Put it in a bottom drawer overnight or stick it to the fridge, as is your preference. The next day, burn it. Have a cuppa and a biscuit, then go forth and write again.

9. Try not to burn bridges, especially while you're standing on them

Pretty self-explanatory.

If you're having a bad experience with a publisher or another writer or bookseller, etc, unless it's utterly necessary to do otherwise, keep it private. We lose sight of this a lot in a world where we cannot digest unless we Instagram our food (I'm very guilty of this food-related quirk, but hey, the food is so pretty and I never have a fight with the food).

Also, be sure of your facts before you open fire on social media. Every situation is going to be different, sure, and I don't have the bandwidth to cover all the possibilities. But before you light up the flamethrower, take a deep breath. Do your research. Know what you're talking about, have all your facts at your fingertips — don't charge into an argument with emotional shouting when you cannot back up your claims with timelines, evidence, etc.

If a situation is doing your head in: step away. Do not engage. "Don't feed the trolls" remains a very wise piece of advice. Extract yourself from the situation as best you can; you might have to cut your losses, but it will be worth it in the end for your peace of mind. And then, if somewhere down the track someone comes to ask why you cut ties with a particular publisher/writer/agent, etc, feel free to give an explanation or a warning. But be wary of being vindictive (or defamatory) — ultimately that will only damage you if you're spending your time fuming after the event.

And be particularly wary of complaining that no one supported your kickstarter/course/charity anthology/trip that you want to take your chihuahua, Esmerelda, on to the Bahamas. That might well be a cause dear to your heart, it might well be worthy AF, but no one is obliged to pledge funds or write for free or keep Esmeralda in little tiny dog bikinis; it's your passion, not theirs.

And frankly, if you're dressing your chihuahua in bikinis, you might have more problems than I can offer advice on. Just saying.

10. Not everyone who writes will get published and that is okay

Not everyone writes to be published. Not everyone wants to be published. Some write for therapy. Some write for amusement. Some write for the sheer joy of a creative personal pursuit. Some write to save themselves and that's nothing to do with anyone else.

If your writing is a hobby, then good on you! If you don't want to publish, then huzzah! You're doing it because you love it.

It is HARD getting published. It is HARD making a living as a full-time writer. It is HARD to keep going, and there is definitely a weird setting on those of us who do so. We really, really are weird.

11. Random tip for free: not all of this advice will work for all writers

I'm not suggesting it will. These techniques have just worked for me at various times and to varying degrees. Every writer is different.

Try a new technique by all means, but if it doesn't work for you (randomly chosen test period: two weeks) then give it up as it is probably becoming a waste of time, an obstruction to your process, and something that will make you feel (even infinitesimally) like a failure. Experiment but do not become a slave to new techniques — a new technique junkie is just a professional procrastinator by another name. But please note: being a decent human being and a good networker and a helpful builder of community? Not negotiable. They aren't techniques or tactics to be shrugged off coz they're too hard. I'm talking about things like rising early to get in 500 words before breakfast, or writing on your morning commute. You know, stuff that affects no one but you.

So: write.

Keep writing.

We are frail, we are fragile, we are insecure, but we have a core of steel (that's how we survive) so we write and we keep writing. Through everything.

1. Major thanks to Dennan Chew and Kylie Thompson for their feedback.

2. Someone (ahem, Kylie) asked 'Yeah, but how do you actually write through when everything is turning to shit?' And that is a fair question, one that deserves its own post on getting through The Block. And I shall write it one day.

3. 'Perhaps you should check your spelling or find a good and faithful beta-reader.'

4. 'If you write *that* no one will ever love you again, you will be pilloried, PILLORIED I say! Also, your dog will crap in your best shoes, even if you don't own a dog. So it has been written and so it has been foretold!'

5. Update: as of this book it's been thirteen years.

6. Which he talks about in detail at www.petermball.com/?s=write+club

7. Things run a little differently nowadays as we've progressed a lot in our careers, and artist and writer Kathleen Jennings has joined us over the last few years. Pete has added "publisher" to his list of titles so we also discuss projects for that endeavour.

8. You can find the primary article at culturedvultures.com/top-5-networking-tips-for-writers

9. My advice on building an online presence can be found in the next chapter.

Online Presence: Pros, Perils and Possibilities

I often hear newer writers (of varying ages) say they want their writing to speak for itself. They're filled with disdain for publishers who look for an online presence, and utterly scornful of writers who actively and efficiently use social media to their advantage. What I generally say to such writers (after I stop laughing) is that their highfalutin' sentiments are delightful, however, if no one can find their writing/book/them then whatever it says is unlikely to be heard.

Your online presence can be a blessing or a curse, but it's what you make it. Just as fire is an excellent servant, it's also a terrible master. You need to control your own social media persona. I understand the reluctance and the fear, I really do. The internet is a chaotic mess of noise, opinions, cat pictures and porn. So much porn. I didn't have website until I met Jeff VanderMeer in 2009, and he (metaphorically) yelled at me until I caved. Five minutes and one WordPress site later I had an online presence where readers and editors and publishers could — and did — find me. What Jeff said made sense: you've been publishing for three years, readers and editors and publishers are paying attention. They're looking for you; be easier to find.

There are a lot of online options for the writer, so many that I'm only going to touch on websites, Facebook, Twitter, Goodreads and Amazon's Author Central. There are others, but these are the most common right now, and I have a word limit — and you all have lives to get on with.

Your website

You might simply want a fairly static site containing your bio, bibliography, an author photo[1], and a contact page. It's perfectly fine to leave it at that, just keep it current. Few things are more frustrating to a reader who's just discovered your work than finding a site that's not been updated since 2001. One of the most important decisions you'll make is about your time commitment: how often are you going to be online in a professional capacity (i.e. not looking at cat pictures)?

Whatever time investment you decide on, stick to it. Be consistent; if a reader knows there will be new content every Wednesday, they'll be there.

The appearance of your site is critical: keep it clean, sparse and tidy. You don't get a second chance to make a first impression, so your website is your interview suit, not your old jeans and t-shirt with last night's curry stains on it. I love sequins and shiny, flashy things as much as the next person, but not on a website. Your pages should not offend the eye nor strobe in such a manner as to cause a fit. WordPress is an easy program to use yourself, but if you've got the budget (or a friend/partner with excellent web skills) then have someone else build a site for you. Keep in mind it's something you ultimately want to be able to update yourself; you don't want to have to pay someone else over and over.

Make sure you buy your domain name and keep it registered — unscrupulous companies have been known to buy unregistered domains, then try to sell it on or back to you.

Make things easy to find on your site, and don't make people click too many links — the time- and attention-poor will quickly leave.

If you include a blog — essentially a diary — remember this: it is not your private journal. There's a reason that old-fashioned diaries have locks on them: to keep your thoughts, opinions, biases, judgments, and crushes secret. Confidential. Ill-considered over-sharing can lead to places you do not wish to go (unless, of course, you're Belle de Jour, in which case it can lead to a lot of money). Don't whinge about the publisher you've submitted your novel to taking *sooooo* long to get back to you. If they've read the manuscript and liked it, they'll look for your web presence; imagine their surprise. So, before you blog, have a really good think about what you want to put out there.

Work out a schedule of topics you want to talk about; take a day a week to draft them. They don't need to be long, a few paragraphs will suffice. If you want to post excerpts from a work-in-progress, great, but remember: this counts as "published". Don't post your entire novel or short story. Blog about your passions because the fastest way to become bored and boring is to be writing about something you have no interest or expertise in: a medievalist will probably be far more engaging on, say, monsters from the Middle Ages than String Theory.

Be very wary of reviewing books on your site — indeed, be wary of doing it anywhere — because later in your career a scathing review may come back to bite you in the proverbial. Even if you delete a post, it's still out there somewhere in an archive or a screen shot, like a time bomb. Waiting.

What other content will interest a reader? If you write science fiction, repost something from Tor.com. Discuss your craft, your new project. Deploy the occasional lolcat. Interview other writers and promote their books. That's an opportunity for cross-promotion and increasing both your audiences. This is networking, which isn't about being a sucking blackhole of need, but about creating mutually beneficial relationships.

You might also add things like press kits, which are useful for anyone who wants to interview you. It gives them some basic information and, hopefully, means they'll ask more interesting questions rather than the ones already answered in said kit!

Social Media Stuff

Facebook is the place where you connect with family and friends, and say anything, right? No, sorry. Readers will send friend requests. You may accept them because you think 'It's my fans! My readers! My peeps!' Here's the rub: you don't know them. 'Tis a sad fact of modern life that they may well be nutbags and/or stalkers. My advice: make an Author Page on Facebook, which reflects the contents of your website. If you get friend requests from someone you don't know, then direct them to that profile, saying you're sure they'll understand that you keep your personal page for family and friends. If they argue, do not engage. Block them. End of story.

To note: do not send another writer a friend request, then, if they accept it, ask them to Like your page. It's rude and annoying, and besides, authors are not your market. Your online presence is for readers, the book-buying public.

Similarly, Twitter may seem innocuous — how could you offend anyone in 280 characters? Quite easily, recent history teaches. Use tweets to draw attention to competitions or giveaways, appearances, articles of interest, lolcats (I myself am partial to otter pics). Do not start a Twitter war as a challenge. In all things, be professional, even if someone else is being a douche.

A useful little app is Hootsuite, which connects to about thirty-five social networks and allows you to have any blog posts made on your site automatically reposted to Facebook, Twitter, etc. It saves time.

Both Goodreads and Amazon's Author Central allow you to set up professional profiles. Both will connect to a blog, if you run one, and repost your content. Both offer a means to tap into existing communities of readers. Goodreads also lets you do giveaways of your books, which can be very handy, and a great way of showing a potential reader what you do and growing your audience.[2]

A word on self-promotion

One thing which hurts my brain is new writers who spend all of their time self-promoting, devoting their online presence to talking themselves up. But when asked 'What have you written/published?' invariably the reply is 'Oh. It's not finished yet.' Then get off the internet and write something. Writing is the key. Without the writing there is no product. Without the product, what is the point?

Keep it secret, keep it safe

Don't give too many personal details on social media. Don't give out addresses or phone numbers, don't mention your kids' school, or where you work. Don't discuss deeply personal matters. Not to be alarmist, but you don't know who is reading. Mwahahaha. Sorry.

And finally

Your online presence is a signal. You control the signal by controlling yourself. Don't answer bad reviews. Don't engage in flame wars. Don't feed trolls. Don't endlessly self-promote or whine. Keep controversial opinions to yourself unless you wish to paint a target on your chest. Be respectful. Be smart. Be funny. Be kind. Be humble. Think of yourself as an artist who is running a business, not as an artiste who would prefer to starve in a garret in Paris before they create an online presence. Tell people about what you're doing, but do not crow and caper. Again: YOU control the signal.

Further reading

For straightforward, no-nonsense, extremely useful advice on this topic, I'd recommend Jeff Vandermeer's *Book Life* and Cat Rambo's *Creating an Online Presence*. Both are very good.

---

1. Make sure it's recent and not a glamour shot from the Eighties, otherwise nobody will recognise you at festivals or cons.
2. Note: Goodreads giveaways are no longer free and are really quite expensive to run.

Time Moves Differently Here

The thing about writing a book is that it takes so long. And this is not a complaint, merely an observation.[1] This is my personal experience.

Bookering, bookerisation, bookification…

From the first tiny spark that you breathe life into to that moment when you're seeing it on shelves … it takes quite a while.

Firstly, you've got to think about it.

Then you've got to start writing it.

Then you've got to finish it.

Then you've got to edit it.

Then you have to find a publisher who likes it.

Then someone else has to edit it.

Then you've got to re-edit it while setting aside your ego, insecurity, doubts, insanity and periodic urges to shout, 'You maniacs, you blew it all up!' whilst shaking your fist at the sky.

Then you send it back to the publisher.

And maybe they send it back again.

And then you go over this thing again — this thing that

was your most beautiful and favoured child, but which you're starting to suspect is instead a changeling left lying in the cradle by trolls or fairy folk just to fuck with you — and then you send it back *again*.

And then, maybe it *doesn't* come back again.

Because just maybe it's ready ... or as close as it's ever going to be in this world and the next.

So, then you're on to looking at cover designs (if you're lucky you get asked which artists you'd like, and if you're not lucky then oftentimes you're *really* not lucky).

And then you've got to ask people you admire to say nice things about your book for the cover quotes (and that's a special circle of Hell right there, sadly neglected by Dante).

And then you've got to write (if you haven't done it prophetically back in the Beginning of All Things) a jacket summary for the book, to make either a novel or a bunch of disparate stories look enticing. Sometimes that feels very much like you're putting lipstick and a peignoir on a rather large show pig.

And then you're almost there and your publisher says, 'We're almost there!'

Then you realise you need to update your bio, and as you've been doing this gig for longer and longer, your bio gets longer and longer, but you've got to Sophie's Choice your favourite babies ... and suddenly achievements that felt like a lightning strike seven years ago suddenly look a bit cobwebby and you feel unutterably sad (but you'll probably utter it anyway coz writer) ... and then you ruthlessly rework your bio with a sense of nostalgia that makes you a little ill ...

And then you've got to find your author photo, which in my case is 12 years old and I actually look like 72 chipmunks in a trench coat nowadays, and I know I need to replace it but I'll still go with the old photo for a while longer (read: deathbed) ...

Here's another thing:

The above doesn't mention the stuff in life that will throw you off course: love, death, day job, time spent with pets, partners and offspring, breakups and breakdowns, roof cave-ins (actual and metaphorical), bushfires, heavy snowfalls, floods, writer's block.

The above doesn't even factor in the delays that are out of your control: happenings in the life of your editor/publisher that throw *them* off course. Anything from pet surgery to bankruptcy, from broken limbs to scandals of all hues.

But then one day, it's ready. And then everything's urgent. So you have to put aside the new book you're working on and go back to thinking about the old one, which has become a bit like the kid you fondly sent off to boarding school or put on a tramp steamer for a trip around the world some time ago ... and suddenly they demand your attention again.

And again, this is not a complaint.

This is a summary of how it happens for me, every time. This is something new and hopeful writers (who've not yet developed a thousand-yard stare) can read and take pointers from to help them manage their expectations. They'll need it if they keep on this thorny, burning, chocolate-strewn, whisk(e)y-flooded path.

It's different for other writers, of course it is.

But this can give you some idea of what it might be like.

My point?

It's a long game.

It takes patience.

A thick skin.

A warm coat and heavy boots for those terrible Russian winters of the soul.

A doomsday prepper-level stash of chocolate and whisk(e)y to help you get by.

And all this was spawned because my next collection is

almost ready and is demanding my attention. And I had to rewrite my bio. And look at that ancient author photo and say, 'Yeah, one more year'. And thank Past Me who had already written a summary two years ago. And be grateful that I also sought out author quotes two years ago so my soul isn't burning with that particular shame today at least. And be so darned grateful that when I work with PS Publishing they ask me who I want as a cover artist and they listen and that Daniele Serra did the most beautiful illustrations based on my novella *Ripper*.

Anyhoo, that's just my day so far.

May your path be strewn with good things as well as bad, and eighteenth-century fainting couches at reasonable intervals along the way for dramatic sighing and crying, general pausing and power naps.

---

1. If your instinct is to bitterly say 'Well, at least your books are published,' then can I suggest that you don't read any further? The door is over there, don't let it hit you on the way out. This post isn't meant for you.

Awards Don't Matter

ORIGINALLY DELIVERED AS A KEYNOTE ADDRESS AT
GENRECON 2017

Good morning to you all, hungover or otherwise.

My name is, as you might have already heard, Angela Slatter.

I would like to acknowledge the traditional owners of this land on which we stand, for they were this country's first storytellers and we always walk in their footsteps, if not their shadows.

So, I'm here today to address an apparently controversial topic, which causes a great wailing and gnashing of teeth, the occasional beating of breasts, and the rubbing of ashes in the hair.

That topic is awards don't matter.

So, who the hell am I to be telling you this horrible thing?

I thought I'd tell you about the milestones in my career as they relate to awards so you can see my trajectory, not because I'm a narcissist. I don't believe in comparing yourself to other writers, but I also believe that in watching the steps others have taken — be they successful or otherwise — you can always learn something.

My caveat: you can't recreate someone else's career. You can try but it won't work because the planets will be in a different alignment to what they were ten, twenty, thirty years ago. But you can learn strategies that can be applied to other situations.

I've scribbled all my life, but 13 years ago I made the decision to embrace poverty, self-doubt and a diet of 2-minute noodles and become a writer. I knew I needed training, particularly in matters of structure and building convincing characters, so I did a Grad Dip in Creative Writing ... then to improve my work yet again I did a Masters (Research) in Creative Writing ... then because I apparently am a glutton for punishment I did a PhD in, you guessed it, Creative Writing.

In those thirteen years since I've written and published eight short story collections (two co-written with Lisa L. Hannett), three novels (the third one is out next year), two novellas, over one hundred and fifty short stories and articles about writing.[1] I was one of the inaugural Queensland Writer Fellows and the Established Writer-in-Residence at the Katharine Susannah Prichard Writers Centre in Perth. I have been awarded four Arts Queensland career development grants, one Copyright Council career development grant, one Copyright Council CREATE grant, and this year I got an Australia Council New Work grant. So if you want to ask me about applying for grants over the weekend, please do so.

I have also won some awards.

So, what Happens When You Win an Award?

Firstly, Kelly Link, writer extraordinaire and international treasure, tries to kill you.[2]

Helen Marshall, another extraordinary writer, joins in —

which is especially awful because she's Canadian. I think she had her citizenship revoked for that one.[3]

So, for me, the awardening began with the shortlistening. The first story I had shortlisted for an Aurealis Award was "The Angel Wood" and that was in 2007, three years after I'd started writing for realsies.

I was shortlisted again in 2008 and 2009.

In 2010 I published my first two short story collections, *The Girl with No Hands and Other Tales*, and *Sourdough and Other Stories*. Both were shortlisted for the Aurealis Award, *The Girl With No Hands* won. *Sourdough* was a finalist for the World Fantasy Awards. That year I also won Best Fantasy Short Story with Lisa Hannett at the Aurealis Awards for "The February Dragon".

In the time since I've had something shortlisted for the Aurealis Awards every year.[4] I've also won four more Aurealis Awards.

In 2012 I won a British Fantasy Award for Best Short Story for "The Coffin-Maker's Daughter". I was the first Australian to win this award; and that's when the award-effect kicked in. There was a lot of print media coverage, the news made it to the radio and even the television. That's when overseas publishers started looking for my name in earnest. That's when I started getting emails about my novel — surely I was writing a novel? Wasn't I? We'd love to see it when it's done.

The BFA got me new readers both at home and overseas. I began to get requests for reprints from places like Russia and Bulgaria and Japan. So, you can see that there was some effect.

It also brought me to the attention of Jo Fletcher of Jo Fletcher Books, part of Hachette International. She was one of those publishers asking where my novel was ... ultimately she did end up as my publisher.

In 2014, I won a World Fantasy Award for *The Bitterwood Bible and Other Recountings*, which is the prequel to the *Sourdough* collection, even though I wrote it afterwards ... so perhaps *Sourdough* had prepared the way. I certainly knew I had readers out there who wanted more of that world.

In 2015 I won a Ditmar for *Of Sorrow and Such*.

In 2016, my debut novel *Vigil* was shortlisted for the Aurealis Awards, and also for the Locus Awards in the US — despite not having been released there — for best debut. This week, *Vigil* was longlisted for the Dublin Literary Prize.

It all seems so easy, doesn't it?

None of this tells you how many words under the bridge, how many tears, how many times I've thrown myself on the eighteenth-century fainting couch and howled that I simply cannot go on any longer. It doesn't reveal the financial distress, the broken relationship, the number of times I've neglected my family and friends because I was on deadlines. Because I was caught up in a story that bodily took me away from the living, breathing fleshy folk around me.

The groaning awards shelf (or: the shelf of groaning awards)

The lovely Dr Kim Wilkins launched my second novel in July this year and made a joke about my groaning awards shelf. She asked if I woke up in the morning, looked at it, and thought: 'Fuck, I'm awesome!'

The answer is no. The answer is that I have to dust the damned things.

But! Awards can do things for your career.

If there's prize money attached — and we always live in hope — then there's a chance that we can pay the rent for a while longer, buy a better bottle of whisk(e)y, stock the pantry with more two minute noodles against the lean times, and just maybe buy a new pair of shoes or underpants before our old ones disintegrate.

There's marketing value. It doesn't hurt your bio to have the words "award-winning author" in there, but please make sure you *are* actually an award-winner before you put that in your bio. Please remember that everything is Googleable nowadays.

It can get you the attention of an agent or a publisher. At conventions or conferences hosting award ceremonies, these folk will appear in the bar with a bottle of Veuve Cliquot in hand if you've just won an award.

Maybe a boost in sales — awards garner media attention, especially if it's a slow news day.

A word of warning: don't tell a writer who has won an award that they're lucky.

There is a point to all of this!

There are three things I want you to take away from today.

1. WINNING AWARDS NEVER MAKES YOU A BETTER WRITER.

In fact, it can give you a complex. It can make you fearful that you will never write anything so good again.

2. LOSING AWARDS DOES NOT MAKE YOU A WORSE WRITER.

I have lost awards and it's never affected how or why I write.

Conversely, it may well drive you on to greater heights ... but you should be striving to write better purely for the challenge of being a better writer — not because you're craving external validation.

3. Awards can be useful marketing tools, but your career will *not* die without them.

They are not and should not be your end game.

I said before don't compare yourself to others. You are a different writer. You can't be Neil Gaiman, because we've already got one and he's rather good at being Neil Gaiman. Don't be the next Neil Gaiman — be the first YOU.

Write the best thing you can. Write the words that make your heart sing — maybe someone else will like the tune. Maybe not. You are not owed an audience. You're not owed awards.

You can't influence the judging panels of awards; you don't know what the competition is like. Sure you wrote the best book you could, but you know what? So did someone else.

At the end of the day, awards are basically Russian Roulette for the Soul. If you write in expectation of them you are setting yourself up for disappointment. Personally, I think writing is such a hard endeavour anyway, why put a new obstacle in your path? The fact is that you might never be published let alone win an award.

So, when I say awards don't matter, what I'm trying to give you is perspective.

If you are writing to win awards, then you need to readjust your ideas or settle in for a lifetime of heartache over something you cannot control. Some of you are simply going to be folk who have that tendency anyway in all aspects of your life — good luck to you, I can offer nothing except the name of a couple of good therapists.

Concentrate on the important thing, the one true thing we have: our words. Write your stories. Write your books. If others want to come along for the ride, then that is wonderful — love that, enjoy that.

When you're dead and dust, you won't leave behind awards — because they'll be buried in the mausoleum with you — and they can't be studied or interpreted or enjoyed. They meant nothing to anyone but you for the brief span you were on the planet.

You'll leave behind your books and that's your legacy.

————————————

1. Update: in the three years since I gave this address, it's now four novels, ten short story collections, two novellas, one collection of microfiction and over 200 short stories and articles on the craft of writing.
2. Please note that Kelly Link did not *really* try to kill me.
3. Please note that Helen Marshall is still a Canadian citizen even though she *did* try to kill me.
4. Update: until 2018.

You Are Not Your Writing

OR HOW TO INTERPRET/DEAL WITH WRITERLY REJECTIONS

I've written before about rejections and how to handle the dent they make in your self-esteem, and I think it's advice that bears revisiting from time to time. One thing any writer needs to develop (apart from mad writing skills and the ability to respect the deadline) is a thick skin. Not everyone is going to like your writing. Some folk will love it, some will loathe it, some will feel neither here nor there about your hard-won wordage — the only thing you can control is yourself and your reaction.

The thick skin doesn't mean that you listen to no one — after all, if someone's correcting your spelling (and they're correct), it's not a matter of your artistic integrity being attacked. Be grateful and gracious, say 'thank you'. Don't be embarrassed, even if the person is a bit of a douche and is trying to make you feel embarrassed — that's their damage, not yours, their insecurity, not yours.

The thick skin means that you keep on writing even after you receive a rejection. I do know people who've given up after their first rejection. Don't be one of those people. Write in spite of the rejections because you should always be writing your story — your first draft — for you. You are your first reader, your first audience member after all. We never learn anything without trying and failing — the greatest teacher in the world is failure. Writing is hard, submitting it to another's gaze is hard, suffering the slings and arrows of outrageous editors is hard; but the important next step is to work out what went wrong. One of the ways you can do this is to read your rejections. Now some writers will laugh and call this "rejectomancy" — a form of scrying as dodgy as peering at the entrails of pigeons — but really there are genuine lessons to be taken away.

So I give you, the **Hierarchy of Rejections**.

The Bad Rejection

The bad rejection can be a sign of a few things: you've sent your sexy nurse story to a gardening magazine; you've sent it off without checking it for spelling and grammatical errors; you've written 'Dear Sir' to an editor who is female or non-binary when a simple Google search would have given you this info. This is also a lesson to research markets and read submission guidelines *very* carefully. Chances are you may well get a bad rejection from an overworked, underpaid, very tired and impatient editor.

Or it is possible the editor is simply not accepting any more submissions, or stories of a particular type. You might have missed the deadline. There's also the possibility that your story sucked. It might be a mostly invitation-only anthology with just a few open sub spots, which means you're competing against a lot of other writers (please note: this is not a reason not to try — by all means submit, it's good practice and editors may well start to remember your name in a positive fashion).

No rejection should ever say, 'Please hand in your

pencil/pen/quill/stylus/laptop at the door and never, ever write again,' but the sad fact is that sometimes the bad rejection may well be rude or mean. Maybe you got someone on a bad day — you didn't do anything wrong, you just got caught in the jet stream of an editor's bad mood (donut shipment didn't arrive; failure of a project; pet death, etc); or the intern who's doing the slush reading has an agenda. You don't know what's happening in other people's lives, so keep a little perspective.

I once got a rejection letter from the editor of a leading spec-fic magazine that did not mention my story at all, but did offer quite a lot of personal abuse because I had provided an email address for notification of rejection/acceptance in order to save trees. This editor was so moved/offended/drunk that he typed this rejection letter personally, used his own envelope, schlepped to the post office, paid for the stamps himself, and roundly abused me for *forcing* him to do this. Have I ever submitted to that magazine again? Will I ever submit there again? If asked/begged for a story by that magazine will I ever say, 'Yes'? The answer to all three questions starts with an N.

The Fair to Middling Rejection

This is your standard 'thanks but no thanks' letter. It is also that sort of rejection *most* rejections are. I know I've talked a lot about the Bad Rejection but that's because it's the one everyone's scared of. The Fair to Middling doesn't say you're a bad writer. It just says not this story, not now. Maybe not ever. Maybe you've chosen the wrong market. Maybe you need to revisit the story and do a bit of flensing. Maybe it was just not quite right. And once again, some of the reasons listed in the bad rejection section may apply. But do not be downhearted, nor vow never to submit to that magazine again. Keep trying. Don't assume this rejection is worse than it is — it's the common or garden rejection.

The Hopeful Rejection

This is the letter that is almost the same as the fair to middling rejection, except in it an editor asks if you'll consider re-working the story, with no guarantee of acceptance. Depending on the extent of the re-writes, give it some thought. Work out if the time investment is worth it for the pay day, and for the time it will take away from working on other stories. And consider whether this re-working can be a good learning experience for you in terms of craft and editing.

The Best Rejection of All

This is the gold standard of rejection letters, the one that says, 'Okay, not this story, but please send another.' What this means is, 'This particular story is not for us, but we like your style and ability so much that we want to see something else from you — yes, you! Yes, this is an invitation to **YOU**. And you know what? This shows we have noticed your work; we will remember your name and, with any luck, you will now get out of the slush pile a little faster.' These are all good things, dear reader-writer; these are not cause for depression. I have known some writers to get a rejection like this and think, 'Well, that's a total rejection.' No, it's not. The door has not merely been left open, but someone has also made cookies and the beverage of your choice.

In Conclusion

Don't just accept one rejection and assume that's it for your writing career — your skin cannot be that thin, your ego that fragile. How many rejections are too many? How long is a piece of string? If a tree falls in the forest does anyone hear it? These are questions with either no answer or an infinite variety of answers, all of which may be right, wrong or a little of both.

How much persistence do you have? Because the **best friend of talent is persistence**. Personally, I give a story twenty rejections — it's an arbitrarily chosen number. It gives me time to get a story across a variety of markets. If it gets the boot from all twenty then I look at re-writing or re-purposing the story. Sometimes the rejection letters help with this because sometimes you get that rarest of things: the rejection letter with feedback telling you **why** the story was not right for them. These are rare because editors of magazines, journals, anthologies, etc, don't generally have time to provide feedback on every story they get. Nor should they have to do so. You want feedback? Join a writing group.

The main thing to remember is this: **your writing is not you**. At the beginning of your career especially, a rejection feels like someone saying your baby is ugly. You may well be tempted to wander around the house doing an Agnes Skinner impersonation: 'A dagger! A dagger through my heart!' The greatest danger is reading a rejection letter and only picking out the negative bits and then translating that negative part into self-loathing: 'I'm a bad writer! My stories suck! I'll never make it! Waaaaaaaaaaaaaaaaah!' It's okay, you get to do this for fifteen minutes — time yourself, then move on. Do it in the privacy of your own home; do not howl online. Then return to writing. Send the story straight back out.

And a golden rule? Do not reply to a rejection unless it is to say, 'Thank you for taking the time to consider my work.' 'Thank you' goes a long, long way. Don't argue with the rejection. Don't try to get the editor to reconsider. Don't write back rejecting the rejection. Don't blog about the rejection, naming and vilifying the editor — if you're going to do that, then just save some time and shoot yourself in the foot right now (off you go, we'll wait). Take Neil Gaiman's oft-quoted advice on rejections. My favourite part is 'The best reaction to a rejection slip is a sort of wild-eyed madness, an evil grin, and sitting yourself in front of the keyboard muttering "Okay, you bastards. Try rejecting *this*!" and then writing something so unbelievably brilliant that all other writers will disembowel themselves with their pens upon reading it, because there's nothing left to write.'[1]

Remember that every writer at some point suffers rejection — you're not alone. And remember that it will happen throughout your career. You will never get to a point where no one dares reject you — and you shouldn't want to because rejections keep you sharp, keep you learning, keep you trying.

---

1. Gaiman has much more to say about rejections at his blog: https://journal.neilgaiman.com/2004/02/on-writing.asp

The Writing Life: A Really Big Echo Chamber

Here's the thing about being a writer: we're all terribly insecure to one degree or another. Although we've chosen a solitary profession, preferring largely to spend time with imaginary friends rather than flesh and blood ones, we still want some attention. Some sign that we're not writing into a yawning void. Some sign that someone's read our work and, just maybe, liked it … or at least didn't hate it. We release a book and wait … and wait … and wait.

And we wait.

Then maybe we get despondent and we howl a little bit. Maybe throw a little pity party involving an alcohol of choice or a lot of chocolate and marshmallows, or an unwise combination of all three. We put on that crushed and crumpled party hat that we stole from a niece/nephew's fifth birthday party, which we grumbled loudly about wearing, but secretly took[1], thinking 'I've a use for this!'

It's one of those conical hats, with iridescent swirls of colour and no real discernible pattern; it's got the last remnants of the multi-hued paper streamers still pouring out of the little hole in the top; and it's got a chin elastic that has long since given up the ghost, but which you keep coz it just about holds the hat on your great melon of an adult skull.

You may even have snookered away one of those party whistles that makes a noise between a honk and a kind of baby elephant trumpeting. And you sit around the lounge room in your underwear, hat on head, whistle drooping from your mouth like an unlit cigarette, and you look at the author copies of the book you poured so much love into and you just feel sorry for yourself.

We've all done it, but like most experiences we actually need to learn from it and move on — otherwise we become trapped in the vicious circle of writerly wah-wah-wah.

Here is the thing about books and the size of the splash they make: not all books carry the same heft and so when they get thrown into the book pond, their ripples all travel different distances.

Things that affect book reception include:

1. Whether you're a Famous Author, or a Semi-Famous Author, or a Famous-In-Your-Own-Circle Author, or a Newbie Author.
2. Whether you're with a big traditional trade publisher with shitloads of money to throw behind book launches, book tours, high-end ARCs, promotional packs, etc.
3. Whether you're with a small independent press that simply does not have the resources to do the things that option 2 does.
4. Whether you, as an author, are prepared to take on some of the responsibility for promoting your book yourself — that includes activating your networks to get books reviewed, running competitions on your own website to give away copies of your book, seeking out places that will

run interviews with you in print or on radio[2], raising your profile by writing articles about, well, anything. Maybe some aspect of your writing process? Or something you researched for your newly released book that people might find interesting? Frankly, if you won't work to sell yourself and your book, you're asking for a book death knell.

Wah! I hear you say, as you gnash your teeth and beat your breast — possibly also throwing on a fetching number in sackcloth and rubbing ashes into your hair — I am not with a big publisher!

You don't need to be.

I am with two small publishers.

I do all 4 things listed in point 4.

I also stay in contact with my publishers and we make sure the books in question are going to a whole range of awards — even if it doesn't get shortlisted, there are still a bunch of people who've read the book that might not otherwise have seen it. We make sure the books go out in a regular and dignified fashion to the handy list of reviewers from around the world that we've pulled together — so, while there may not be a gigantic explosion of a bajillion reviews of my book all at the same time, there is a steady series of reviews over a period of time, which means at different times different audiences learn about that book. *Sourdough and Other Stories* and *The Girl With No Hands and Other Tales* were published in 2010 — they are still getting reviewed now in 2013 **and** still selling.

Small press is about a long game and strategy — and it involves you, as the author, not just leaving everything to your publisher. Be realistic about the cycle and you will find reviews coming up at odd times, like very pleasant depth charges. And don't just focus locally — send books across the seas, into the big wide world.

Maybe one day you'll be with a big, rich publisher who will take care of everything and all you will need to do is write your golden words and bathe in caviar whilst scoffing champagne with marshmallows in it. But until that day, as a writer your job does not stop when you write "The End".

So, my friends, *until that day* be patient, be wise, be strategic.

And remember, you are not lost, you are not alone, you're not writing into a vacuum — the reaction hasn't been heard because you're writing in a really, really big echo chamber and the sound just hasn't come back to you yet. Keep writing and keep making **productive** noise.

Oh, and conduct a little ceremony and burn the party hat.

Not the whistle though, keep that — it makes noise, so we know where to find you.

----

1. After all the cake had been eaten and the creepy magician clown had finished his show.
2. A small indie radio program is still giving you a promotional medium you wouldn't otherwise have had.

Thank you

Thank you to those folk who've done early reads of these posts over the years: Ron Serdiuk, Dennan Chew, Lisa L. Hannett, Angie Rega, Suzanne J. Willis, Kathleen Jennings, and Kylie Thompson, and to Peter M. Ball and Brain Jar Press for ideas so crazy they just might work.

About the Author

Angela Slatter is the author of the supernatural crime novels *Vigil*, *Corpselight* and *Restoration* from Jo Fletcher Books, as well as nine short story collections, including *The Girl with No Hands and Other Tales*, *Sourdough and Other Stories*, *The Bitterwood Bible and Other Recountings*, and *A Feast of Sorrows: Stories*. She is also the author of the novellas, *Of Sorrow and Such* and *Ripper*.

Vigil was nominated for the Dublin Literary Award in 2018, and Angela has won a World Fantasy Award, a British Fantasy Award, a Ditmar, an Australian Shadows Award and six Aurealis Awards. She has recently signed a two-book deal with Titan Books for *All The Murmuring Bones* and *Morwood*, gothic fantasies set in the world of the *Sourdough* and *Bitterwood* collections.

Angela's short stories have appeared in Australian, UK and US *Best Of* anthologies such *The Mammoth Book of New*

Horror, The Year's Best Dark Fantasy and Horror, The Best Horror of the Year, The Year's Best Australian Fantasy and Horror, and The Year's Best YA Speculative Fiction. Her work has been translated into Bulgarian, Chinese, Russian, Italian, Spanish, Japanese, Polish, French and Romanian. Victoria Madden of Sweet Potato Films (*The Kettering Incident*) has optioned the film rights to one of her short stories ("Finnegan's Field").

She has an MA and a PhD in Creative Writing, is a graduate of Clarion South 2009 and the Tin House Summer Writers Workshop 2006, and in 2013 she was awarded one of the inaugural Queensland Writers Fellowships. In 2016 Angela was the Established Writer-in-Residence at the Katharine Susannah Prichard Writers Centre in Perth. She has been awarded career development funding by Arts Queensland, the Copyright Agency and, in 2017/18, an Australia Council for the Arts grant.

Find her online at www.angelaslatter.com

facebook.com/angelaslatterauthor
twitter.com/AngelaSlatter
instagram.com/angelaslatter

Also By Angela Slatter

Thank You For Buying This Brain Jar Press Chapbook

To receive special offers, bonus content, and info on new releases and other great reads, visit us online at www.BrainJarPress.com

CPSIA information can be obtained
at www.ICGtesting.com
Printed in the USA
LVHW030123120121
676186LV00006B/155

9 781922 479044